THE CUBIES' ABC

Mary Mills Lyall

[ZHINGOORA BOOKS]

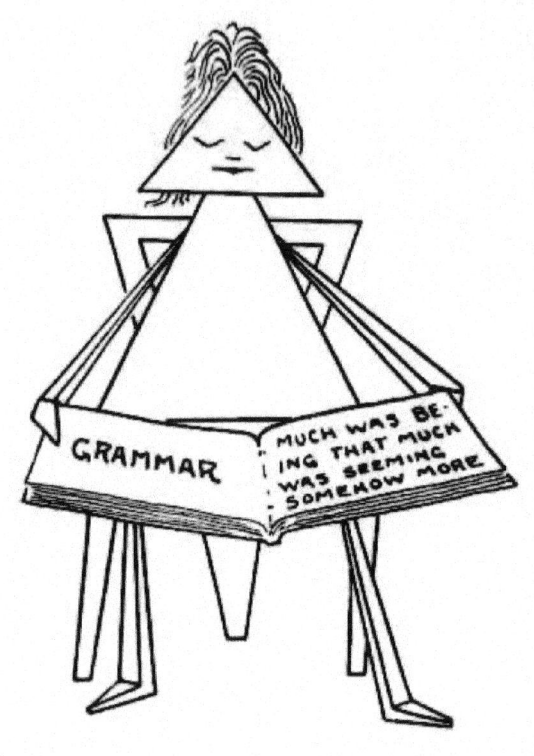

**GRAMMAR MUCH WAS BEING THAT MUCH WAS
SEEMING SOMEHOW MORE**

◣THE CUBIES'◢

 is for Art in the Cubies' domain—

(Not the Art of the Ancients, brand-new are the Cubies.)

Archipenko's their guide, Anatomics their bane;

They're the joy of the mad, the despair of the sane,

(With their emerald hair and their eyes red as rubies.)

—A is for Art in the Cubies' domain.

 is for Beauty as Brancusi views it.

(The Cubies all vow he and Braque take the Bun.)

First you seize all that's plain to the eye, then you lose it;

Next you search for the Soul and proceed to abuse it.

(They tell me it's easy and no end of fun.)

—B is for Beauty as Brancusi views it.

 is for Color Cubistic ad libitum—

(Orange and blue, yellow, purple and green.)

"Throw them all on your boards," Cubies say, "then exhibit 'em!"

There'll be no colors left, if we don't soon prohibit 'em!

(Watch them at work and you'll see what I mean.)

—C is for Color Cubistic ad libitum.

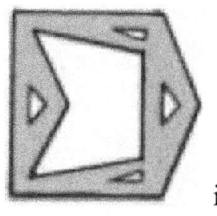 is for Duchamp, the Deep-Dyed Deceiver,

Who, drawing accordeons, labels them stairs,

With a lady that must have been done in a fever,—

His model won't see her, we trust, it would grieve her!—

(Should the stairway collapse, Cubie's good at repairs.)

—D is for Duchamp, the Deep-Dyed Deceiver.

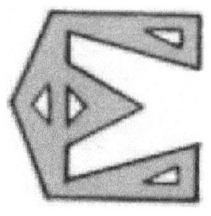's for the Ego, intense and Exotic,

Enjoyed by a Cubie, and quaintly Expressed

In a lachrymose face with a gaze idiotic

When seen on the canvas.—It's really Quixotic

To offer one's soul to the Cubical test!

—E's for the Ego, intense and Exotic.

's for the Future for which Cubies hanker;—

To Hals, Perugino and all that old crew

They give up the Past without envy or rancor,

While saying in tones than which naught could be franker:

"Come, move on,—it's our turn! They have finished with you."

—F's for the Future for which Cubies hanker.

 is for Gertrude Stein's limpid lucidity,

(Eloquent scribe of the Futurist soul.)

Cubies devour each word with avidity:

"*Alone* words lack sense," they affirm with placidity,

"But *how* wise we'll be when we've swallowed the whole!"

—G is for Gertrude Stein's limpid lucidity.

 is for Henri's young Red Top, the shaver

Whom Cubies regard with aversion and spite.

His life-like appearance has won their disfavor:

"He might walk right out of the picture!" they quaver,—

"Why, only to think of it fills us with fright!"

—H is for Henri's young Red Top the shaver.

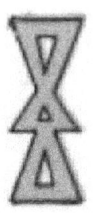 's for the Cubies' Immense Intuition,—

"The only real need of an artist," they say:

"Without it we all would go straight to perdition!"

Between you and me, I've a sneaking suspicion

The Cubies themselves appear well on the way!

—I's for the Cubies' Immense Intuition.

 's for the Jam in the Cubies' headquarters,

And the Jar that they gave us, the first time we met;

And that same Jar of Jam from across the blue waters

Is quite unexcelled among those the importers

Have wafted us over the ocean as yet.

—J's for the Jam in the Cubies' headquarters.

 's for Kandinsky's Kute "improvisations"—

The Kubies abound in delight for his art:

They say there's a Klue to his Kryptic Kreations.

By means of Picabia's deep ratiocinations

Some day we may really decipher his heart.

—K's for Kandinsky's Kute "improvisations."

 is for Life that is "still," as they name it,

Or "nature" that's "dead," as you readily see.

When you think how it's treated, you really can't blame it.

You'd wish, in it's place, *you* were dead. Just the same it

Is shocking how cruel the Cubies can be!

—L is for Life that is "still," as they name it.

's for Matisse's Mam'selle Marguerite,

(With whom all the Cubies are madly in love;)

Her manner is so prepossessing and sweet

That, if she but had them, we'd fall at her feet!

(In her eyes, what a mingling of serpent and dove!)

—M's for Matisse's Mam'selle Marguerite.

 's for the Nudes that the Cubies portray,—

We willingly vouch for their perfect propriety,

Even while some we regard with dismay,—

For instance, the lady as long as Broadway:

With all due respect, we don't crave her society!

—N's for the Nudes that the Cubies portray.

's for Objective and Optical Art,

(The kind we've been used to, these long years gone by,)

Which the Cubie Objects to with all of his heart:

"Make the Object Subjective," he says, "at the start,—

Just a matter of Grammar, as easy as pie!"

—O's for Objective and Optical Art.

's for Picasso, Picabia and Party

(Who deal in abstractions, distractions and such.)

When, with vision chaotic and expletives hearty,

You beg of a Cubie their sense to impart, he

Profoundly makes answer: "In little is much."

—P's for Picasso, Picabia and Party.

's for the Queerness we Stand-patters feel

When Progressive young Cubies start Art reformation.

They're strong on Initiative, praise the Square Deal:

"Though the Cubic is best!" they aggressively squeal;

"Painting things as you see them is rank deformation!"

—Q's for the Queerness we Stand-patters feel.

 is for Reason and poor old Reality,

Once in the fashion, but now obsolete,

Banished forever with grim actuality.

Now the sole law is one's own personality—

Find its Cube Root and you have it complete.

—R is for Reason and poor old Reality.

 is for Schamberg's fair dame at her 'phone,

Conversing with G. Stein, the Futurist scribe.

The Cubies, eavesdropping, hear Gertrude bemoan:

"This one feeling many far seeming alone,

The bluer the bliss the redder the bribe!"

—S is for Schamberg's fair dame at her 'phone.

 's for the Type of Tree Chabaud's erected.

The Cubies insist it's as useful as fair

For a game that they play when they're feeling dejected,

(A use which not every one would have detected,)

Lassoing the branches with rings of their hair.

—T's for the Type of Tree Chabaud's erected.

's for the Union so Utterly Useless

Uniting the members that make up the whole.

Against it the Cubies wage war that is truceless:

"Such rage for convention," they cry, "is excuseless!

Away with cohesion, and set free the Soul!"

—U's for the Union so Utterly Useless.

 is for Villon's musicianly lady

(With charm evanescent and Visage remote.)

The picnics he gives in his orchards so shady

Account for his hit with the Cubes. I'm afraid he

Will spoil them completely for plain table d'hôte.

—V is for Villon's musicianly lady.

's for Woolworth, the building so stable,

(Erected with nickels and dimes by us all,)

Which Cubies paint writhing from cellar to gable,

Distinctly resembling the Tower of Babel,

Some decades ago, just preceding its fall.

—W's for Woolworth, the building so stable.

 is the Xit, Xtremely alluring

When Cubies invite us to study their Art;

And the Xquisite pain we are sadly enduring

The while they protest, with an air reassuring:

"Of course this is merely a diffident *start*!"

—X is the Xit, Xtremely alluring.

's for the Yawn overcoming each Cubie

At sight of a painting not done in his style:

"If a man doesn't use all the colors, from ruby

To sapphire and emerald and topaz—the booby!—

To look at *his* canvas is not worth one's while!"

—Y's for the Yawn overcoming each Cubie.

 is for Zak's summer-time composition;

The Cubies regard his plump hills with delight.

They are somewhat fatigued after this exhibition

And tempted to slumber; so, with your permission,

We'll tuck them in snugly and bid them goodnight.

—Z is for Zak's summer-time composition.

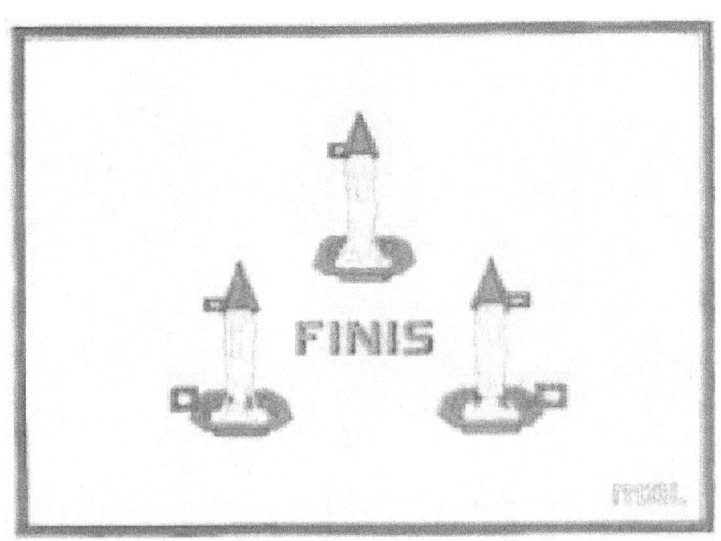

A B C

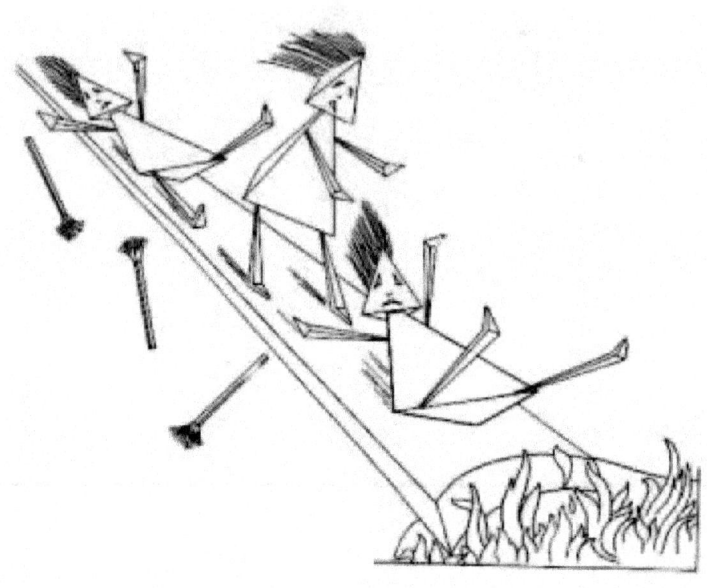

The End